Swing Trading Using the 4-Hour Chart

Part 1: Introduction to Swing Trading

Heikin Ashi Trader

I0482311

Tabe of Contents:

1. Why Swing Trading?

Most newcomers to the stock market try their luck with day trading. By this, is not saying anything wrong. You can earn a lot of money indeed with day trading if you are good at it. IF! The problem is that many aspiring traders significantly underestimate the difficulties in day trading. I just list a few on:

In this short timeframe you are competing with hundreds of thousands (mostly young) traders who are very well trained and equipped with the most advanced technology possible.

A quite significant competition you can expect from the so-called algorithms. In other words, you fight expensive computer programs that were developed by the best minds.

More competition you can expect from the lack of volatility in recent years. It happens more often that the typical trading markets, such as the E-mini, mini Dow future, EUR/USD and crude oil go sideways all day only to suddenly make a big jump without warning. Do you have the right position at this very moment?

Your biggest competitor is not at least yourself. Do not underestimate the psychological pressure when day trading. Many traders have run aground using this method. Even if you have a moment of success, it does not mean that this must always be so.

If in spite of these drawbacks you still want to day trade; then go for it!

Unlike day trading, position trading with daily charts or even weekly charts is a much more comfortable way to make money in the stock market. And, frankly, I would recommend most people to use this method.

But beware! Again, there is also a lot of competition, here! Here you have to compete with the major operators: investment funds, insurance companies and hedge funds that speculate in medium-term time frame with stocks, indices, commodities and currencies.

Those highly capitalized pools could, for example, have the idea to sell in large numbers the stock you just bought. Not because the stock has suddenly become bad. It could be, for example, that they need money for another investment. Or, they need it in order to pay their disgruntled customers. You see, even "investing" is not that simple. You may as well call the stock market a snake pit and you would not even be in the least, exaggerating. Is there no alternative?

I think there is. This alternative I call **swing trading**. It is a style of trading that takes place in a timeframe that is too slow for day traders and too fast for investors. In other words, in this timeframe, there are very few professionals trading. You will also hear nothing about it in the press. When was the last time you ever read an interesting article in the newspaper about swing trading? Probably never...

What timeframe do I mean? The charts that swing traders usually use are hour charts, or even better, 4-hour charts. In some cases, swing traders also work with daily charts. This is a period which falls between the investor and the day trader. You sit as if between the chairs, and that's good, because here you are almost alone.

2. Why should you trade using the 4-hour chart?

There are good reasons to work with the 4-hour chart. The smaller time frame, such as the 5-minute chart or 15-minute chart (typical of the day traders), are not representative of the Money Flow. What the big money does, you do not see here. However, you can clearly see it on the 4-hour chart. A technical pattern has a much higher information value here. This indicates rather, who controls the market at the moment: the bulls or the bears. You want to know this as a trader, right?

Unlike most other traders who like to work with candlestick charts, I use the **heikin-ashi chart**. This chart type has several advantages: The trend is more visible thanks to the visual smoothing of the candles (unlike Candlesticks). The strength of the trend is visible by the size of the candle and the occurrence of pins (long shadows above or below the body of the candle).

In other words, the heikin-ashi charts illustrate the imbalance between supply and demand very well and even show the inflection points clearly. Thus, they are an excellent tool to identify the capital flows in the markets. The example below from the Dow Jones index illustrates this.

Figure 1: Dow Jones, 4-hour chart, HeikinAshi

The 4-hour chart shows the "swings" very clearly. Those movements usually last a few days. Upswings (white, rising candles) and downswings (black, falling candles) are clearly seen in this example of a HeikinAshi chart. To illustrate this, I will show you now the same segment of the Dow Jones index in the candlestick representation:

Figure 2: Dow Jones Index, 4-hour chart, candlestick

I hope you can see the difference. Of course, you can work well with the candlestick charts. But, I prefer the visual presentation of the HeikinAshi chart against that of the candlesticks. I like it when I can detect at first glance whether a market is in an uptrend or a downtrend.

On candlestick charts you will often get contradictory signals. In an uptrend, suddenly black candles could appear that could give the trader the impression that the trend is over. Such false signals are mostly filtered out on the HeikinAshi chart. This is an advantage not to be underestimated.

This example also shows very clearly what experienced traders know for a long time: market movements usually last 3 to 5 days. After the market has had a rally for 5 days, it mostly calms down again. It then forms a consolidation or sideways movement.

In the above example, the upward movement took place in three waves that you can identify very well thanks to the white candles in the HeikinAshi chart. These waves lasted about 24 hours (or eight 4-hour candles). The intermediate correction phase (usually black candles) also lasted about eight candles. Overall, this movement took the Dow Jones five days. For three days, the Dow was in an upward motion and two days in a correction movement. This pattern you will see over and over again.

As a swing trader you want to, of course take advantage of these swings. The 4-hour chart visualizes these movements very well in the context of the current market situation. Incidentally, swing trading works even if the market is not in a trend, but in a volatile sideways movement. The example below shows such a phase.

Figure 3: S&P500, 4-hour chart, HeikinAshi

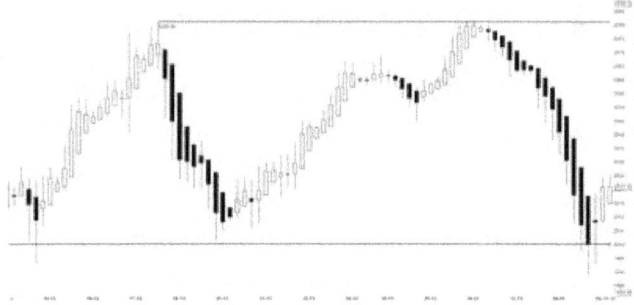

Figure 3 shows a sideways trend in the **S&P500 index**. I have indicated the upper and lower limits using a horizontal line, as these were significant in this example. The bottom line, which is also called the support, falls exactly with the round number 2000. Such price levels in the financial markets have an important psychological meaning and are respected by many traders as well as by institutional market participants.

It is therefore no coincidence that the market is experiencing support at this level. That is, there are many willing buyers waiting there to catch the market up as soon as it reaches this price level. As a swing trader you should attach greater importance at such "psychological marks". Typically, you will see that the market in the first or the second contact "turns" at such levels.

Timing

A further important reason to work with the 4-hour chart is the timing. For day traders timing is everything. For swing traders applies: The direction has to be right. You should give the market a few hours' time or days to develop. So, it does not have such a strong role, whether you have purchased the Dow at 16,500 or 16,550. The major thing is the right direction.

As a swing trader you need to also cope with periodic counter-movements. It may well be that the market temporarily runs 30-50 points against your position. This should not get you out of your position. As a day trader you cannot afford that.

Your wins are also bigger if you do swing trading. You will mostly profit from those unexpected movements, of which I spoke earlier using this method. You just cannot know in advance when they will appear. But, that's not so bad. As a swing trader, you can wait until the market makes its decision.

You usually have several hours of adequate time to think about an entry. You do not have to buy now and straight away. I also recommend using limit orders when working. By so doing, you can build your position calmly, after you have done your analysis.

If you buy via market order (or sell market when you go short) you agree to the current market price. This is usually not the best price to enter a position. Often, it is worth placing your limit order 50 points lower, if you want to buy. It may well be that the market seeks this level again before heading in the desired direction.

Last but not least: You do not have to sit all day in front of the screen. Many newcomers to the stock market find this of course very exciting to watch the rise and fall of prices. But, this has nothing to do with making money.

As a swing trader you make once a day an analysis of the markets you trade. You put your orders in and you are ready for the day. It is my unique experience that the results are better if you do not constantly check your positions. I know that in the era of tablets and

Smartphone this might be a challenge. But, if you have traded for a while, you will be able to confirm this experience.

It is best to accompany your long position (or short position, when you go short) with an OCO-order. Your position is thus automatically protected by a stop loss order to limit the losses and to realize the profits through an automated take profit order when the target is reached.

Either one or the other order is triggered. The respective outstanding orders will be automatically closed by the system. The rest you are better off leaving to the market if this particular trade will be a winner or a loser. You can close your PC or laptop and do something else.

This procedure is called "Set and Forget." The Trader places his buy limit, which is automatically accompanied by a predetermined stop-loss order and a take profit order. He thus determines his maximum risk and at the same time identifies a price level at which he wants to realize the profit.

Figure 4: Waiting short position in crude-oil futures

To illustrate this point, I want to show you an example of a short position in the crude-oil futures. The horizontal line is a resistance level at US $ 50.20, where I want to sell (i.e. to go short). As you can see, the market when I made the screenshot of the chart had not yet reached this level. So, my sell limit waited until this event occurred.

At the same time I had at $ 50.60 (black line above) this sales order accompanied with a stop order and at US $ 48.80 (black line below) I had put a take profit order. At the moment in which my sell limit at $ 50.20 would be triggered, the other two orders would be automatically activated. So I knew that I had a risk of $ 0.40 on this trade and that I could win $ 1.40. This corresponds to a risk-reward ratio (RRR) of about 1:3, which is great.

Should one of the two orders which accompany my sell order be executed, the other order is automatically cancelled. As a trader I need do nothing but wait and see how the market will decide. This kind of serenity to the market is what you should develop as a swing trader, because you can only do your best with your analysis. Ultimately it is the market that decides, whether you will make a profit or a loss with your next trade.

If you always enter trades with a good RRR, then this good habit will be reflected sooner or later in a positive trading result. Through a qualitative good selection of trades (which is the subject of the second book of this series), you can improve this result further.

3. Which markets are suitable for swing trading?

In principle, you swing trade in every market. Shares are good instruments, since they have some very strong fluctuations. But, not everyone is good with shares. For example, I'm not good with shares. It certainly has to do with the fact that the stock market closes in the evening only to open again the next morning.

This is not always to your advantage, because the closing price of a day is not per se the same with the opening price of the next day. Very often differences occur, that are called overnight gaps or price gaps. This can occur naturally to your advantage, but also to your disadvantage. It really gives no joy when you get up the next morning, and the stock that you bought yesterday is 5% lower.

The alternative for a trader who wants to avoid big price gaps in shares is: only trade markets. What do I mean by this? You should trade general markets instead of shares. This can be equity indices (Dow Jones, DAX, NASDAQ, and S&P500), commodities (gold, silver, oil) and currencies (euro, dollar, pound, yen ...).

If you trade "markets" instead of stocks, you might indeed occasionally also end up experiencing price gaps, but they mostly are much smaller than gaps that occur in stocks. The reason is simple. If you trade the Dow Jones for example, you are invested not in one, but in 30 companies. The Dow Jones is nothing but a basket of 30 major American companies.

The different price gaps of these 30 shares equal most out, so, the overnight gaps in the Dow Jones index are mostly moderate. If you ever experience as a trader a period in which you see gaps of 5% or more in stock indices price, then you should seriously consider a trading break.

Such extreme gaps mostly appear during periods of increased volatility, as for example in 2008 this was the case during the financial crisis. Fortunately, these periods are usually short and do not occur too often on. But you cannot rule them out, which is why you should always keep an eye on the **VIX.** The VIX is the abbreviation for CBOE Volatility Index. This index expresses the fluctuation of the US stock market index S&P 500.

Figure 5: VIX, 2006-2016

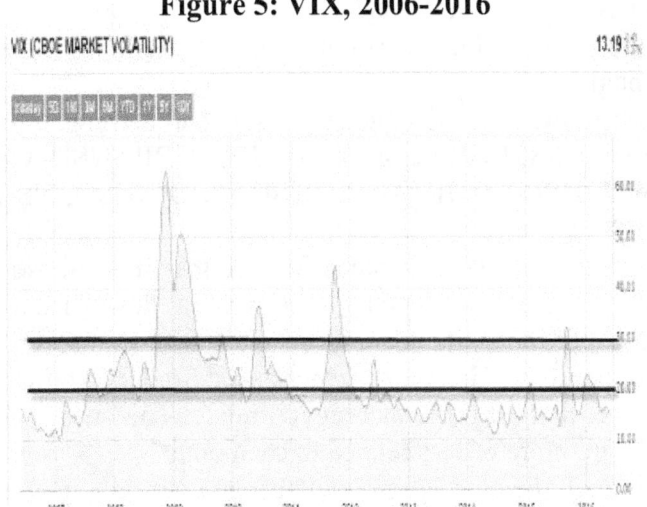

Figure 5 shows a chart of the VIX from 2006 to 2016. The two horizontal lines on the chart are the indicator of volatility. Values below 20 are considered "low volatility", while values above 30 are classified as "high volatility". At the time of the screenshot, volatility has been 13.19, which was almost regarded as historically low. Clearly visible are the years in which the volatility rose far above the 30 mark. These were, in this case in 2008 and 2011.

Not coincidentally, these phases are consistent with the 2008 financial crisis and the euro crisis of 2011. In November-December 2008, the VIX reached extreme values of over 60 points. These were the weeks of the Lehman Brothers bankruptcy. The world economy was on the brink of a disaster, and I recommend to you, if such a phase should appear again in the financial markets, to temporarily cease trading.

I myself run my swing trading with a basket of indices, commodities and currencies. Here is the list:

Indices: DAX, Dow Jones, SP500, Nasdaq100

Bonds: Bund futures (futures on the German 10-year bonds).

Commodities: WTI Crude Oil, Gold and Silver

Currencies: EUR / USD, EUR / JPY, GBP / USD, USD / JPY, USD / CHF, AUD / USD, NZD / USD, USD / CAD

That's a total of 16 markets. Believe me: If you observe these markets every day, you have a fairly accurate sense of what is happening on the financial markets at the moment. The more experienced traders know, of course, that all these markets correlate. This means that they are more or less related to each other.

Although the correlations can change over time, you can still set up some rules that apply generally:

1. Stock indices often highly correlate. When the American markets rise, you will see mostly that the

Asian or European indices do this as well. The three major US stock indexes Dow Jones Industrials, S&P500 and Nasdaq100 can safely still be called the drivers of the world's stock markets. When these three are in a downward trend, the other indexes have a generally hard time countering this.

2. The US dollar is still the most important currency in the world. If the US dollar rises, usually the other major currencies such as Euro, Australian Dollar, British Pound, New Zealand Dollar, Canadian dollar or Swiss francs are going down.

3. A strong dollar is usually unfavorable for commodities such as gold, silver or oil, and vice versa. This correlation can of course change temporarily. But, you will see that the correlation sooner or later sets in again.

On the subject correlations a whole book is to be written. If you know the three mentioned rules, you are already ahead from the majority of market participants, who know nothing about it. If you want to deal with, for example, the correlations among the currencies, I recommend this site. You can find information on correlation change in the major currency pairs on an hourly, 4-hour and daily basis.

4. Which Instruments are Suitable for Swing Trading?

For most markets on my list you can trade with an **ETF**. ETF stands for exchange-traded fund. This is an investment fund that is traded on an exchange. If you know nothing about ETFs, you will certainly find enough information by doing a simple Google search. There are also excellent e-books on the subject.

Most ETFs that reflect the major financial markets have a good liquidity. You get tight spreads (buying and selling rates) and you usually have no problem if you wish to resell your position. Here is a small list of the most popular ETFs. The underlying markets I have written next to it.

- SPY: S&P500
- QQQ: NASDAQ
- GLD: Gold

If you plan to operate your swing trading with **futures**, then you will have to deal with price gaps, because futures markets have opening times. Usually price gaps are smaller in markets than that in equities. Major markets do not often open up the next day with large gaps.

Many swing traders employ CFDs for their swing trading business. CFD stands for Contracts for Difference, so they are instruments that track the price movement of a market 1 on 1. CFDs have similar to futures, a very high leverage. To illustrate this, I will give you an example from the DAX.

- Note that CFDs are not permitted in the United States.

Suppose you want to buy 1 CFD contract on the DAX at a price of 10,000 (DAX Stand 10.000). Depending on the broker you have to pay a 1% margin for this contract. This means that it is enough if you have 100 Euros (or British Pound) to your account so that you can buy 1 contract. In that case, you move 10.000 Euro with only 100 Euro (Pound) as your stake!

If the DAX now goes up to 10,500 points and you sell, you will realize a gain of 500 points or 500 Euros (British Pound). Most CFD traders I know usually have no more than 1000 Euros in their account. If you realize a gain of 500 points on this trade, you multiply your capital with 50%. And you do this with only one trade!

As long as you win, this is great of course. However, you should always have in mind that this leverage is just as valid if you lose. If you take, in this case, a loss of 500 points, you have set already 50% of your capital in the sand! Definitely not a great feeling...

So you should think carefully about whether you want to start your swing trading business with leveraged instruments. Often, it is better to tackle the matter in a more conservative manner and to trade first with ETFs, which have usually little or no leverage. Your wins might be smaller here, of course, less, but your losses will also be limited.

If you want to eliminate the risk of price gaps completely, you should only trade currencies. Currencies will be traded during the week, 24 hours. The market opens on Sunday evening and closes next Friday evening. There are therefore no surprises.

You should then close all open positions before Friday night. Usually you can on Sunday evening or Monday morning reopen them if you are convinced that your position should continue to be held after the weekend.

When trading currencies, you can also calculate your risk optimally. You only risk the distance between the entry price and your stop-loss order.

This is an important advantage. With most brokers you can also control the position sizes remarkably. I recommend starting with the so-called microlots. These are 1000 US $ -Lots. Every slight change of a Pip will make or cost you US $ 0.1 only here. If you lose 50 pips, then you have only lost US $ 5. This is safe to handle.

5. Swing Trading Setups

Now we come to the most important part of my method: the setups that I trade. Again, I try to keep it as simple as possible. I will show you some examples of setups that I trade often. A setup is basically no more than a certain pattern on a stock market chart. Since certain patterns emerge again and again, traders have agreed on certain terms over the years. Most of them are so simple that every layman trader can understand them immediately.

Incidentally, I am only talking about the entry opportunities here. Where the stop should be placed, and where I see a target in a specific market situation, this will be the subject of the third book of this series on swing trading. The title of the third book is therefore: "Where do I put my stop?" So I will start first with the easy part: where do I get in?

A. Support and Resistance

For some traders this approach might be too simple. The fact is that support and resistance levels are still among the most powerful setups that the market can offer, provided you know what you're doing.

The terms, support and resistance are derived from technical analysis. Analysts speak of a support when they discover a price level in the chart, where the market repeatedly rotates upward. This means that at the support, the buying pressure obviously increases driving prices upwards again. When resistance occurs, exactly the reverse happens. Here, increasingly sellers emerge, who push prices down.

The reason why there exists such a price level may be different. In equity markets, it often happens that a larger trader only starts to buy once a certain price level is reached. A good trader can take advantage of this fact by also buying at this price level swimming with the big sharks, as long as they are driving prices upwards.

In stock indices or in the currency markets this is also the case of course. But, here, often purely technical chart considerations play a role. The general markets are more technically oriented markets. Mostly tens of thousands of traders are involved worldwide. They all watch the same price tags on their charts. No wonder as if by miracle hand that prices turn at certain levels, and this happens several times often in succession.

A swing trader, who is able to recognize these pivot points, may well develop a profitable strategy. He buys the support and sells at the resistance (or goes there short). I want to illustrate the concept with some examples.

Figure 7: Crude Oil, 4-hour chart, HeikinAshi

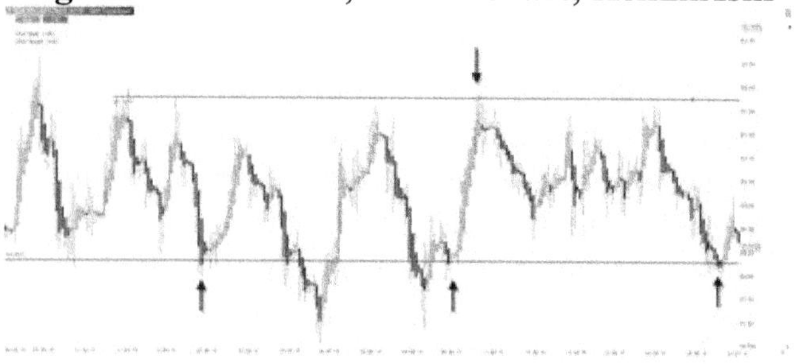

This example from the **Mini Crude Oil Futures** illustrates the concept pretty well. The oil price seems to fluctuate between two areas and is traded in a recognizable sideways movement. This is called a **"range"**. Clearly visible is the upper price level at US$

61.74, where crude repeatedly turns down (upper horizontal line). Such price level is what the analysts call resistance.

Below arrived at US $ 58.28, the price turns upwards again (lower horizontal line), so technical analysts speak of this as the support. It is but typical for the oil market that price movements somewhat "exaggerate". We see this in this example, especially at the support. It was immediately breached down twice. A few hours later, crude returned back to the range. How to trade such exaggerations or "fakes" I will describe in the second part of this series on swing trading.

Such ranges can occur in all markets. The price is equally caught between two levels at which it's larger players either buy (support) or sell (resistance). A good swing trader can exploit this fact by buying support, with target price resistance and sell the resistance with price target support. Protective stops the Trader places best slightly below the low of the previous candle or above the high of the previous candle for short positions.

B. Double top and double bottom

An interesting entry point is the so-called double top and double bottom. A double top is formed when the price reaches after an initial consolidation the high of the previous rise again but cannot break up. The prices fall back, because all market participants know now that buying pressure has been diminishing.

Figure 8: EUR/USD, Daily Chart, HeikinAshi

This example of a double top in the EUR/USD occurred between March and May 2014. The euro had recovered in the months after the so-called "Euro crisis" and was heading the round 1.40 mark against the US dollar. Here the euro formed the double top in Figure 8 (both arrows).

It was interesting to see that in the second point of the double top (right arrow), the first high from March 13th was indeed overcome shortly on 8th of May 2014 but the day candle closed under the first high. The EUR/USD approached in the course of the trading day the level 1.3992, but did not make it to the round mark 1.40.

Such details are what swing traders should pay attention to. This information tells the trader that massive sell orders must be waiting at the round mark 1.40, which should prevent the euro from overcoming this level. The result was a clear sale of the currency pair in the following days and weeks. It was equal to 500 pips lower.

But, that was not all. This first downward move was merely the start of a further massive downtrend in EUR/USD which eventually led the pair to below 1.05. In other words: The double top was good for a total of 3500 pips! Who would have gone short here and have put a protective stop something above 1.40 would have generated a fantastic return.

Although these opportunities are rare, they exist, and I believe that every swing trader should try to at least take some of these movements. A single trade of this category can make your trading year.

The reverse situation occurs with a double bottom. In the example below, from February 2016 E-mini future (Figure 9) prices had reached a first low, whereupon they recovered temporarily. In a renewed relapse they reached the first low a second time, but here sellers were no longer able to push the market down. Result: Prices again began to rise and the double bottom was perfect.

Figure 9: E-mini, daily chart, HeikinAshi

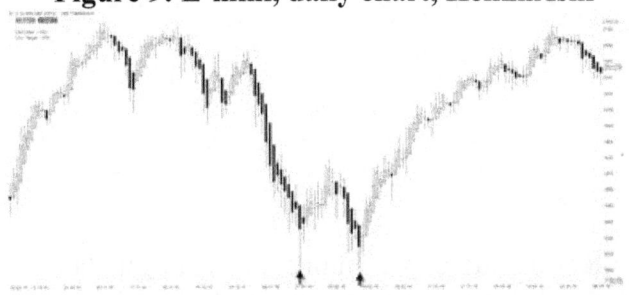

This example from the future on the American stock index **S&P500** is an exemplary standard. On January 20, 2016, the price reached a first low at 1804. In the subsequent trading days they recovered though a little, but came back a second time, forming a second low on 11 February 2016 at 1802.50. Now, this second low was indeed "something" deeper than the first one. Throughout the day the E-mini recovered and formed a so-called reversal candle. This is a candle, which marks a new low marks but closes near the day's highs during the trading session. Sellers therefore failed to keep prices low.

The next day, the E-mini formed a spinning top. This is a formation with a small body but with long shadows above and below the body. Such candle indicates an equilibrium situation between buyers and sellers. At least the selling pressure was gone, and the chance that we were dealing with a double bottom was now a given.

Figure 10: FDAX, 4-hour chart, HeikinAshi

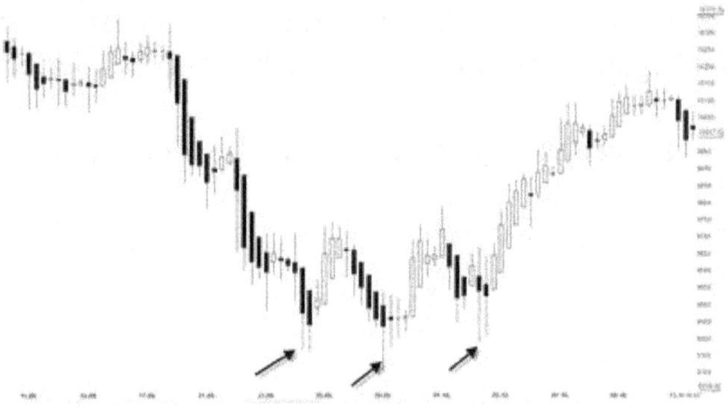

Excellent trading opportunities are also triple bottom as shown in Figure 10 in the **FDAX**. This bottom formation was quite interesting, because the second low (medium arrow) was slightly lower than the first and the third. This signals to the trader, on the one hand, that the lows were really explored here and on the other hand buyers always stood ready at this level to catch up the market.

One recognizes this fact in the long shadows among the candles (three arrows). This makes these candles to the aforementioned reversal candles, which suggested a 180% rotation in the other direction, which actually happened after the third low. The buy signal came after the first white candle after the last reversal candle (third arrow to the right).

Figure 11: SMI Futures, daily chart, HeikinAshi

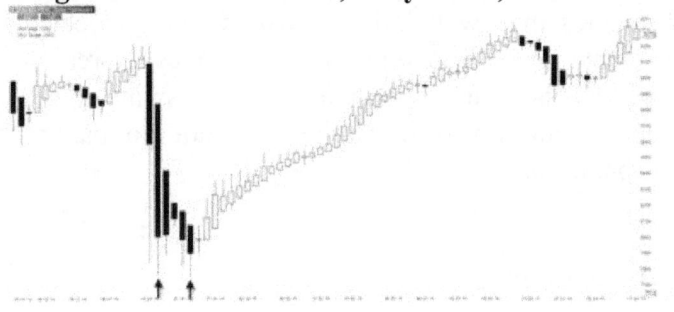

Extraordinary events sometimes bring even unusual opportunities. Some traders will remember the so-called "Swiss Franc Tsunami" of 15th January, 2015. That was the date on which the Swiss National Bank lifted the coupling of the franc to the euro at a stroke. The franc rose in price within half an hour by 20%, which represents a landslide movement in the Forex market.

This of course had its consequences on the Swiss stock market. Figure 11 shows the SMI-Future, so the future on the Swiss equity index of these days. After the index had calmed in the days after the crash, a double bottom (arrows) was built on the HeikinAshi chart, which provided an extraordinary opportunity. In the following weeks, the index recovered from this event completely. The losses were made up every day, which the HeikinAshi candles prove impressively.

It is quite worthwhile for a swing trader to observe markets which have, for example, experienced a decent crash. It is crucial that you find a formation that suggests a reversal, as this was the case in this example of the

SMI. Eventually, markets recover even from the deepest blows that they receive.

For equities, this is not always the case, because unlike indices that represent a whole basket of stocks, shares of companies may well fall to zero, as some spectacular bankruptcies of economic history have impressively proven. This is also a reason why as a swing trader, I trade general markets. Markets do not go bankrupt. Companies do.

C. Breakouts

Granted, breakouts have fallen into criticism in recent years and rightly so. The argument is: there are too many false breakouts in order to still trade this pattern profitably. I understand this argument, but I would also make it clear that one cannot equate all breakout situations.

In the second book of this series on swing trading I will go into details on the phenomenon of the so-called false breakouts or "fakes" and show how you can even develop a very profitable trading strategy that meets the realities of today's markets requirements.

There are certain breakouts that you can better lie to the left. One of my rules is: The longer the foregoing consolidation takes (the more tests the market takes to break a support or a resistance) the more important a potential breakout becomes. In other words: Five trials are much more significant than three. When I see something like that, then I am interested.

Figure 12: EUR/JPY 4-hour chart, HeikinAshi

This example of the currency pair EUR/JPY (Euro - Japanese Yen) illustrates hopefully, what I'm saying. We can see that the pair tried several times to overcome a flat running resistance line. There were a total of 8 attempts, until the pair succeeded (arrows from the top). The breakout was not, as so often spectacular in such cases. On the contrary, the pair hovered for hours over the line and repeatedly made short trips underneath (4 arrows from bottom to top).

The swing trader therefore had all the time to think of a good entry, which has at some point also paid out. At its peak there were up to 400 pips to pick up!

D. flags

After strong trend movements, temporary consolidations are not uncommon. The market comes to rest for a short time and then continues its trend movement. That is why we speak in this case of trend continuation patterns. These formations can take different forms, but the best known are probably the so-called **flags**.

The image of the "flag" is therefore used by traders, because the formation looks actually like a sort of flag.

The previous uptrend is considered as the flagpole, while the short opposing consolidation can be seen as a flag. Accordingly, there are not only flags, but also pennants. In a pennant the consolidation does not proceed in a parallel trend channel as the flag but runs on a tip.

If you speculate on the trend continuation, you expect that this trend is still strong and not over. A flag suggests this at least. In contrast to range trading the trader here speculates really on the big trends, which of course occur in the stock market from time to time.

Flags are excellent opportunities for a trader who is able to identify them on a chart. There are traders who deal exclusively with this pattern and only trade flags. Flags in an uptrend are simply called bullish flags. In a down trend they are called bearish flags. Mostly they run contrary to the main trend like in figure 13 below.

Figure 13: FDAX, 4-hour chart, HeikinAshi

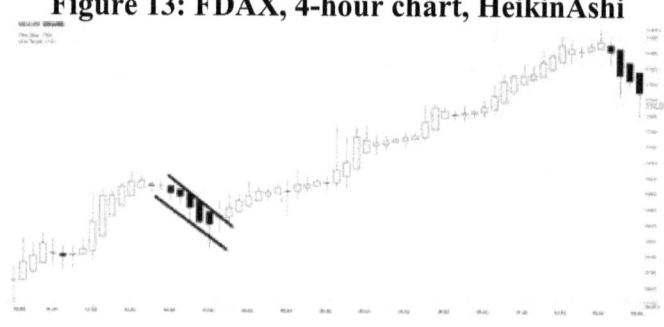

This example in the FDAX illustrates the concept of a bullish flag very well. We see a clear upward trend on the left part of the chart. Most HeikinAshi candles are white. The apparent opposite movement occurs which lasts a few hours. Here the candles are black, as the market seems to go back down temporarily. This consolidation phase lasts only briefly. After a while the FDAX begins to rise again.

Usually, flags extend in a small trend channel. The break of the upper line of this channel provides the buy signal. Bullish flags are therefore also interesting because they usually occur in strong trend phases, as in this example. The market should continue its trend soon after the end of the flag. The trader can secure his position with a stop slightly below the trend channel of the flag.

With Flags, traders usually achieve a good risk-reward ratio. A position bought at 10,900 points could have been protected with a stop of 100 points. But, this swing trade yielded 1500 points! In other words, the trade generated an extraordinary risk reward ratio (RRR) of 1:15!

In such an index as the DAX this is a huge profit, which never came under threat. During this buying wave after the flag, the HeikinAshi Candles remained permanently white. The exit took place then 1500 points higher after the first black candle.

Such opportunities happen on a 4-hour chart again and again. I therefore believe that this timeframe can be very profitable if the trader has the patience to wait for such occasions.

6. Money Management

Money management is certainly one of the most important tools for a trader. In terms of risk, of course, it should be noted that this is handled differently by each trader. A rule of thumb is that you should never risk more than 1% of your capital per trade.

There is a good reason for that. Suppose you are wrong 10 times in a row (which is not uncommon, when it occurs rarely). With a 1% risk you will lose 10% of your capital. You must now make 11% profit, to get back to break-even (to 0). That's doable.

But, if you risk 5% per trade (which many beginners like to do), and you have 10 losses in a row, already half of your capital is gone. It goes without saying that this is extremely detrimental to your psyche. Plus the fact that you now have to make 100% profit to get your stake back.

Another approach, which I would recommend is to simply specify a fixed amount as the maximum risk per trade. You could, for example, agree with yourself that you would risk no more than $100 per trade. That would be your current comfort zone. Later, when your knowledge and confidence level has increased, you can still increase this sum.

7. Trading Diary

I would recommend a trading diary for any trader (not just beginners). I have kept one such diary of my trades over the years. Why? You get after a while, very interesting statistics regarding your own trading behavior.

A diary tells you after a series of trades, for example, in which markets you are good and where you are less so. Isn't that interesting information? And does it not make sense rather to focus on your strengths?

I am good in the Swiss franc and the Canadian dollar. The British Pound however, I do not touch. Here my stats are not good at all. When trading FDAX and the euro I do relatively well, but I'm top in Dow Jones. If you have such data, it's hopefully clear which markets you should trade.

There is also a psychological gain. A diary gives you security. The daily and weekly monitoring and review of your trades gives you stability and continuity. This is especially important when things are not going so well. You can then look in your diary and see that there have been such periods before. And there will be again ... It simply belongs in the business of trading.

Here's an example from my own trading journal:

Figure 14: Trading Diary

Datum	Underlying	Position	L/S	Entry	Stop	Risk	Exit	Points P/L	P/L Euro
08. Apr	Gold	1	L	1576,6	1579,9	376	1579	-30	-342
09. Apr	DAX	1	L	7703	7690	195	7698	-4	-60
	EUR/USD	150.000	S	1,3034	1,306	274	1,3046	-12	-137
	Dow Jones	1	S	14615	14640	285	14612	3	34
10. Apr	BTP	1	S	111,82	112,15	495	111,97	-15	-225
	EUR/USD	150.000	S	1,3076	1,311	388	1,308	-4	-46
11. Apr	EUR/JPY	100.000	S	130,57	130,68	106	130,68	-16	-106
	EUR/USD	100.000	S	1,3121	1,3136	114	1,3136	-15	-114
	WTI	10	S	94,36	94,7	258	94,04	33	251
	Gold	7	S	1556	1563	372	1561	-50	-266
12. Apr	Silver	1	S	27,53	27,7	194	26,36	117	1334
	DAX	10	L	7802	7770	320	7889	-13	-130
	Silver	1	S	2707	2740	376	26,36	71	809
W15								65	1002

I made 13 trades during that week. Of these, no less than 9 ended up as loses! But, this is a complete normal week. You see, it wasn't looking very good until Thursday, 11th April. But then, on Friday I had two very profitable gains in the silver market. These 2 winners made the difference for the whole week. But if I had not limited the number of loses I experienced, no profit would have shown up. Now the Balance + € 1,002 are not bad despite the fact that over 60% of the trades were lost.

8. What is it all about?

I have deliberately chosen this example from my trading journal, because it illustrates the art of trading quite well. Most of the 13 trades this week brought little profit, or were even loses. This is completely normal and a daily occurrence. But, sometimes you get a really good chance like these two silver trades on Friday. These two trades are what made the difference.

You will not get these trades generally, if you had not taken a disciplined approach in the days before. The most important psychological problem you have as a trader is that you never know when these winners will emerge. But one thing is certain: those of us who are well prepared for any of these opportunities will take those opportunities!

I wish you success!

HeikenAshi Trader

If you have questions, please contact me at: pdevaere@yahoo.de

Glossary

Bond: Interest-bearing securities, also annuity or Obligation

Breakeven: Point at which total cost and total revenue are equal

Candlesticks: Coding of price changes on the basis of a Japanese analysis technology

CFD: Contracts for Difference

Continuation pattern: Break in the main trend at the conclusion of which previous direction is resumed.

Correlation: Correlation is a statistical measure of how two securities move in relation to each other.

DAX: German stock index.

Doji: Candlestick formation by which the opening and closing prices are at the same level.

Day trading: Daytrading describes the speculative short-term trading in securities. A trader will open a position and within the same trading day close it again.

E-Mini Futures: Futures contract on the American index SP500.

Forex: Forex Exchange Market, international foreign exchange market.

Futures: Futures contract. Standardized contract to buy or sell a specific amount of a commodity at a specified price, on a specified date.

Gap: A price difference between two trading days.

HeikinAshi: "Balancing on one foot" Japanese representation form of price changes.

Indicator: Identification of technical analysis, which is designed to determine price movements of securities.

Limit Order: Order with a fixed price and/or fixed time for the execution.

Liquidity: Describes the extent to which a security can be sold and bought at any given time.

Market Order: A market order is executed on the stock exchange at the best possible price at the time of the order.

Momentum: The momentum informs the investor about the pace and strength of a price movement.

Microlot: A microlot corresponds to a contract of $ 1,000 in a currency pair.

Money Management: Money Management refers to a strategy which aims to control the risk of the securities portfolio by size determination of the individual trading positions.

OCO (One cancels the other): A combination of stop-loss and a limit sale; when either the limit or the stop price is reached, the order is executed and each order clears the other order.

Pip: Percentage in point, the smallest change in the price in currency trading.

Position Trading: A position a trader holds in the long term (months to years).

Range: A clear defined trading range over a given period.

Risk-reward ratio (RRR): The RRR is an indicator of the usefulness of a system. It is calculated by dividing the expected profitability of the maximum loss.

Short position: A trader short is when he sells a position without owning them (short sale).

S&P 500 (Standard & Poor's 500): Stock index comprising the shares of 500 of the largest listed US companies.

Spinning Top: Chart pattern with a small body and long shadows

Spread: The difference between bid and price offer.

Stock index: Measure of the performance of the overall equity market or individual stock groups (e.g. DAX or NASDAQ).

Stop Loss Order: Sell order which is carried out once a certain price is reached.

Take Profit Order: A Take Profit order is used when the market reaches the desired profit rate.

Reversal candle: A reversal candle (also Pin Bar) terminates a previous price movement in one direction and introduces a new price movement in the opposite direction. Close of the candle is mostly at the top.

VIX: The VIX expresses the expected volatility of the US stock market index S&P 500.

Volatility: Standard deviation. Specifies how the price of a market varies

More Books by Heikin Ashi Trader

(Available as e-book and in print)

Swing Trading with the 4-hour chart
Part 2: Trade the Fake!

In the second part of the series "Swing Trading using the 4-hour chart" the HeikinAshi Trader speaks about the phenomenon of stop fishing and Fakeouts as well as the many deceptions that major players and algorithms stage in today's financial markets. These often seem more the rule than the exception.

But these circumstances are what a clever swing trader can exploit by turning the tables. Instead of falling for the many tricks of the Smart Money, he can learn how to identify their tracks in the chart. From this, he can develop a highly profitable swing trading strategy that focuses exclusively on the detection of so-called "fakes". Often, it turns out that the deception of the major players represents just the start of a significant movement. To trade this is mostly high rewarding.

With reference to several examples in different markets and technical chart situations the author follows the traces of the Smart Money. With practice, every trader can locate these tricks on a chart and identify the underlying intentions. Such a strategy would correspond more to the reality of today's markets, instead of trying to beat the market with outdated methods.

Table of Contents

About the Author

Heikin Ashi Trader is recognized worldwide as the specialist in scalping with the Heikin Ashi chart. He has been trading this way for 19 years. He traded for a hedge fund and then went into business for himself as a trader. His scalping book "Scalping is Fun!" is an international bestseller and has been sold more than 30,000 times. You can find more information about his scalping method on his website www.heikinashitrader.net

Imprint

Texts: © Copyright by Heikin Ashi Trader
Swiss Post Box 106287
Zürcher Strasse 161
CH-8010 Zürich
Switzerland